What Is God Like?

Text © 2008 by Beverly Lewis

Illustrations © 2008 by Pamela Querin

Design: Lookout Design, Inc.

Published by Bethany House Publishers
11400 Hampshire Avenue South
Bloomington, Minnesota 55438

Bethany House Publishers is a division of
Baker Publishing Group, Grand Rapids, Michigan

Printed in China.

ISBN 978-0-7642-0466-1

Library of Congress Cataloging-in-Publication data is available.

MY DAD IS LEAVING TODAY for his longest work trip yet. A whole week! I'll sure miss him.

"I wish you could stay home with us," I told him.

"Me too," Dad agreed. "But don't forget—even when I'm not here, God is always with you."

"Is God a lot like you, Daddy?" my little sister, Emily, asked. Well, she *is* only five.

"Not exactly, honey. I'm your father here on earth, but God is your Father in heaven—the Father of us all."

Emily looked confused. "So God's our father, too?"

Dad nodded, smiling at us both.

"We know what you're like, Dad," I said. "But what is God like?"

So Dad set his suitcase down and told us again about our Father in heaven. "He's bigger and more powerful than anyone," Dad began. "And He loves you even more than I do. Can you can imagine that?"

Dad told us many other things about God. Important things I hope we never forget.

"But for us there is only one God. He is the Father.
All things came from him, and we live for him."
1 CORINTHIANS 8:6

It was the hottest day of the year. So after Dad left, Emily and I spent the afternoon in the backyard, playing and splashing each other in our little pool.

"Do you really think God loves us more than Mom and Dad do?" Emily asked.

"Well, they love us a whole bunch," I said. "But no one ever will ever love us more than God does."

"Why not?"

"Dad said it's because God *is* love."

Just then a chickadee called from our tallest tree. The bird's call sounded like, "God loves you—oo—oo...."

I poked my sister. "Hey, listen to that!"

She nodded and giggled. "I hear it, too."

"How great is the love the Father has given us so freely!
Now we can be called children of God. And that's what we really are!"

1 JOHN 3:1

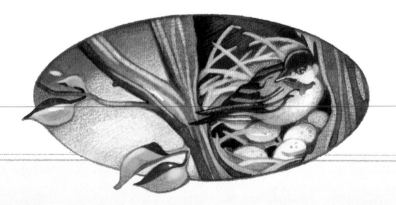

I tried to remember what else I had learned about God.

"The Bible says God is everywhere, and He can see everything," I told Emily. "He's with all the people on the other side of the world at the exact same time He's here with us."

She smiled. "Can He see our cousins clear out in Colorado, right this minute?"

"Yep. He sees everyone all the time."

"Aren't two sparrows sold for only a penny? But not one of them falls to the ground without your Father knowing it. He even counts every hair on your head! So don't be afraid. You are worth more than many sparrows."

MATTHEW 10:29–31

"God must be really smart," Emily said.

"He's way smarter than we'll ever be," I told her. "He even knows more than Mom and Dad."

"More than our teachers, too?"

"Yes," I answered. "He knows everything."

Emily grinned. "Does He know I'm going to spray you right now?"

I laughed and ran. "And He knows what you'll do tomorrow and the next day and for the rest of your whole life!"

"Lord, you have seen what is in my heart.
You know all about me.
You know when I sit down and when I get up.
You know what I'm thinking even though you are far away.
Lord, even before I speak a word, you know all about it."
PSALM 139:1–2,4

"Uh-oh," said Emily. She wasn't smiling anymore.

"That means God knows when I do something wrong, too."

"But He never stops loving you. He forgives you—when you're sorry for what you've done."

Emily still looked sad.

"Hey, I don't always do what I should, either," I said.

Emily smiled again. "No kidding!"

"But God does everything right. He's perfect—there's no one like Him!"

"I forgive those who refuse to obey.
And I forgive those who sin."
EXODUS 34:7

"God is really powerful, too." I said.
"He's the strongest, fastest superhero ever."

"He must be," Emily agreed, "to make the
whole world."

"Maybe it was easy for Him. The Bible says
He opened His mouth and the planets and stars
appeared, just like that."

"You mean like we blow these bubbles?"
I laughed.

"Is anything too hard for God?" Emily asked.

"I don't think so. He's greater than anything
or anyone in the whole world."

"The heavens were made when the Lord commanded it to happen.
All of the stars were created by the breath of his mouth.
He spoke, and the world came into being."

PSALM 33:6, 9

Later, when the sun was sinking low in the sky, Mom helped us build a campfire in our fire pit.

When she went back inside for marshmallows, I asked Emily, "Do you remember the last thing Dad said before he left?"

She shrugged. "You mean, 'I love you two'?"

"Sure. But he also told us to be good and to obey Mom while he was gone."

"Oh, he always says that."

"So it's important, then. God wants us to obey His rules, too."

"Why?" Emily asked.

"Because they're good for us. You know how Dad always warns us not to get too close to the fire?"

She nodded, gazing now at the flames.

"God's rules are like that," I told her. "They warn us to stay away from things that hurt us. Obeying Him keeps us safe and happy."

"I am the Lord your God. Listen carefully to my voice.
Do what is right in my eyes. Pay attention to my commands.
Obey all of my rules."

EXODUS 15:26

Mom let us sleep outside that night so we could see a comet that
was supposed to pass over our town…if we could stay awake long enough.

So I lay on top of my sleeping bag and stared up at the sky. I could see the
moon and a tiny red light Dad had said was the planet Jupiter. Fireflies flickered
all around me, their little lights reminding me of stars.

I remembered Dad saying there are more stars than all the grains of sand on all
the beaches of the world. And that God made them all. He made the world and
all the other planets, the sun and moon…everything.

As I lay there under that big sky, hoping to stay awake for the comet, I tried to
remember everything else Dad had told us about God.

"You are the one and only Lord. You made the heavens. You made even the highest heavens. You created all of the stars in the sky. You created the earth and everything that is on it."

NEHEMIAH 9:6

Emily must have been trying to remember, too, because she asked me, "Do you think God will ever change?"

"Dad says He never will. He's the same as He was two weeks ago and even last year."

"But *we* change." She squinted her little eyes.

"Yes, but God's different. He will be the same tomorrow and next month and a zillion years from now." I grinned at her. "And no matter what, He always loves us."

"The mountains might shake. The hills might be removed. But my faithful love for you will never be shaken."

ISAIAH 54:10

"Always?" Emily piped up.

"Always. And that sure makes me feel safe."

"Do you feel safe out here in the dark?" Emily asked, looking around.

"Yep. And besides, Mom's right inside."

Emily wriggled her sleeping bag closer to mine. "Aren't you just a little scared?"

"Since God is always with us, why should I be? He watches us…protects us, too."

"I will lie down and sleep in peace. Lord, you alone keep me safe."

PSALM 4:8

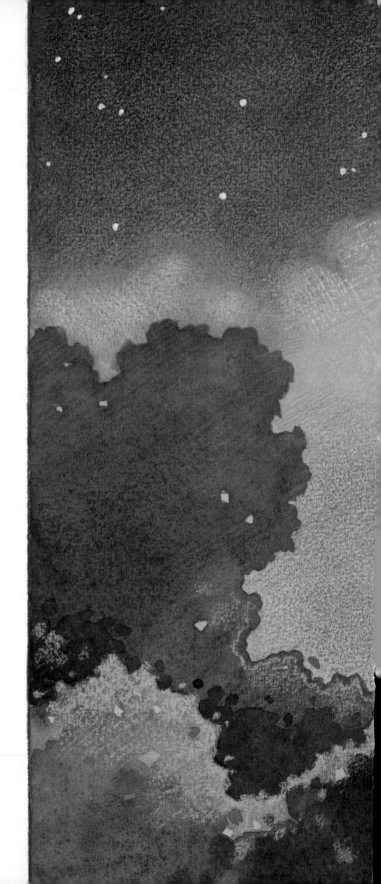

"Does God ever sleep?" Emily asked. "Or does He ever get too busy?"

"He never sleeps, and He's never too busy for us," I told her. "Besides, He can do lots of things at the same time. Dad says God gives us the things we need and never stops loving us."

Her eyes lit up almost as bright as the campfire. "Really? Do you think He has enough love for everybody in the whole world?"

"Sure! And He never runs out."

"You open your hand and satisfy the needs of every living creature."

PSALM 145:16

Suddenly we heard a cry and Emily jumped. But it was only our neighbor's kitty, meowing and crawling under our fence.

"Here, Skittles," I called. "Here, girl!"

She slinked over to us, snuggled down onto my sleeping bag, and began to purr.

"God made the animals," I reminded my sister. "He made kittens, and ponies, and elephants—"

"Even fireflies?" Emily asked, looking up.

"Even fireflies. And every animal is extra special."

"God made all kinds of wild animals. He made all kinds of livestock.
He made all kinds of creatures that move along the ground.
And God saw that it was good."

GENESIS 1:25

Emily smiled, showing off her missing tooth. "And God made me!"

I nodded. "And He knows your name…and all about you."

"All the other kids, too?"

"Everyone in the whole world!"

She wrinkled up her face. "I don't understand how He does it."

"I don't either, but God can do anything."

"You created the deepest parts of my being. You put me together inside my mother's body.
How you made me is amazing and wonderful. I praise you for that.
What you have done is wonderful. I know that very well."

PSALM 139:13-14

Emily reached over to stroke Skittles. "She purrs so loud, I wonder if God can hear it!"

"He hears everything…even when just my heart talks to Him."

"Wow, God must have good ears!"

I had to laugh. "I don't know if God really has ears, but I think He likes it when we talk to Him."

"Do you mean pray?" asked Emily.

"Yeah, and it's really easy. You just say thank-you—for a safe place to live, good food, clothes—and ask for help if you're in trouble or lost. Stuff like that. He's always ready to listen."

"*The Lord is ready to help all those who call out to him.*
He helps those who really mean it when they call out to him."

PSALM 145:18

Emily curled up in her sleeping bag like the cat and yawned. "Why did God make people, anyway?"

"Dad said He wants to be our Friend—the best one we'll ever have."

I started thinking about Dad. Every time he comes home from a trip, his smile is so big. He picks us up and gives us bear hugs. I think that must be how our heavenly Father feels about us, His children.

"Thank You, God," I whispered. "I love You, too."

Right then I decided to try to please my heavenly Father by obeying Him, loving Him, and taking care of the beautiful world He created.

My sister was quiet beside me. I looked over and saw she was sleeping.

For a long time, I watched the sky, still thinking of Dad's words. I couldn't wait to see him again and tell him everything I remembered.

I must have fallen asleep, because I never did see the comet pass over our town that night. I'm just glad Dad took the time to help me see something even better—what God is like.

"Give thanks to the Lord, because he is good.
His faithful love continues forever."

PSALM 107:1

TEACHING YOUR CHILD ABOUT GOD

If your children are like mine were (and like my grandchildren are now), you've already experienced the excitement and challenge of teaching them about our heavenly Father. We want our children to know and love our great and all-powerful God, but how do we effectively teach them about someone we cannot see?

Or *can* we?

Our loving God can be seen in His magnificent creation, in the tender and unconditional love of parent to child…in prayers answered. And in the peace evident in our hearts during difficult times.

There are many ways to illustrate the reality of our heavenly Father to our young ones. But I think the best way is to demonstrate a strong faith in a very real, very loving God in our own lives.

Undoubtedly, the Bible is the ultimate source of information about God and His plan for us. That's why I've selected verses that— along with Pam Querin's exquisite and engaging illustrations—bring God's attributes to life.

As you share this book with your children, encourage them to describe their own perceptions of God. You may be surprised at the expression of their childlike faith. The eyes of their spiritual understanding are open so wide now, and I pray this book will provide ongoing discussions about our wonderful God, for you and your dear family.

Beverly Lewis